Pepper Your Life With Dreams
The Little Book on LifeCoaching and Inspiration

Picerjaw & Co Ltd • Bournemouth • Dorset • BH6 4EQ • England

©PaTrisha Anne Todd 2002
All rights reserved. No part of this publication may be reproduced, stored in a retrieval system, or transmitted in any form or by any means, electronic, mechanical, photocopying, and recording or otherwise without the prior written permission of the publisher.

ISBN 0-9543262-0-2

The right of PaTrisha Anne is hereby identified as the author of this work.

A copy of this book is available on request from the British Library.

Picerjaw & Co Ltd. in Great Britain publishes this edition 2002.

Cover designed by Kathryn Patrick.

Technical support Ben Wilfred.

CONTENTS

Dedication	*'My Ever Loving Heart'* Page ii	
Introduction	Brian Willey ex BBC Executive Producer & Song Writer Page iii	
Foreword	Why and how this little book came into being Page iv - v	
Chapter 1	LifeCoaching and what it is Page 1	
Chapter 2	Inspiration and what it means Page 11	
Chapter 3	Insightful expressions penned by PaTrisha Anne Page 15	
Training	Your opportunity to learn the Craft of LifeCoaching Page 87	

DEDICATION

Written with love and dedication to my two Darlings,

Mum and Dad.

It is because of these two wonderful people my life and this book have been created and the journey towards my destiny, full of love and guided inspiration has begun.

I love you both.

'My Ever Loving Heart'

INTRODUCTION

The poet W B Yeats quoted in his biography, *"...all life weighed in the scales of my own life seems to me a preparation for something that never happens."* To how many of us does that sentence reflect our own lives? Sadly there are far too many to whom may apply - in some cases a far too aptly. It is such persons that PaTrisha Anne had in mind when she put her own thoughts and dreams on paper - words of love and advice to inspire and encourage.

Because her book is full of expressions, it caused me to recall words of wisdom that other had written - and one very relevant phase comes from the American poet Ralph Waldo Emerson, who wrote,

"Nothing great was ever achieved without enthusiasm."

It is true, so obviously true, and if we all applied those words to our own lives we could make a great difference to ourselves and to all those around us. By reading the words contained in this little book you may just find the inspiration and enthusiasm for the life that you have been seeking and has thus far escaped you.

Happy reading and a happy life.

Brian Willey
(Ex-BBC Producer and Song Writer)

FOREWORD

Was it by chance that you chose to pick up this book and read it? Or maybe it's part of your destiny.

It has always been my ambition to share my love of words and inspiration with others like you. This book allows me to do just that and offer you the little gems of inspiration that have coached me through times of crisis.

Tragedy strikes when it's least expected. My children have been pillars of strength throughout the past few months. With gentleness they have cradled me in their arms showering me with love and affection when I needed them most.

All of the expressions contained within these pages have been written with feelings of care, affection and sensitivity of one who has struggled for years to WIN in the game of life. It's my belief that you'll treasure this book filled to the brim with jewels of reflection. Please think of it as a gift from me to you, even if we have never met.

FOREWORD

Enjoy what you read and take it all in with an open mind. Simply open the book and read what you see. Do it randomly. These principles are part of me and have on many an occasion brought a smile to my face, a tear to my eye or given me the courage to carry on.

Have fun with the language and *Pepper Your Life With Dreams*.

PaTrisha Anne

CHAPTER 1   LifeCoaching

LIFECOACHING AND HOW IT WILL BENEFIT YOU

I have over the past half year taken the time to write this section to guide and coach using the concept of LifeCoaching towards a lifestyle you truly desire.

Many of you will already be familiar with the concept of LifeCoaching. However, I strongly recommend that you read this segment with an open mind, in fact read the whole book. After all LifeCoaching is based on elegance and about making the choice to step up to the starting line and play the game of life to win!

Whatever your thoughts and standards are on the attainment of a prosperous and fun filled lifestyle I earnestly encourage you to reach out and claim your destiny. You are already standing on the threshold of your desired lifestyle. So why not begin to coach yourself from today? Begin now by using the essence of these words and follow through. You can also draw inspiration from the insightful expressions contained within chapter 3.

As with all worthwhile results quality teaching and constant application of those tools and principles give you what you want. The only draw back is who can you

CHAPTER 1   LifeCoaching

can you trust enough to guide you along this path of exploration, plus make it fun?

I would opt for self. That's right, self. Once you have made the decision to turn your daydreams into reality you'll discover how to make them happen, anything could happen. LifeCoaching is limitless.

Throughout time many a wise man and woman have made statements that human beings are the masters of their own destiny.

Do you know why that is? I'll tell you.

Any individual becomes the master of him/her self by utilising the power to programme their own subconscious mind.

That personal power is locked within. LifeCoaching is the key for that lock. LifeCoaching takes each of us by the hand from right here and now to where we believe we want to be. That journey towards goal is never ending.

CHAPTER 1 — LifeCoaching

We all have a free will. We can all navigate our own lifestyle. However, the actual application of putting into action the desire takes courage. This courage comes from hunger. Yes that's right, hunger. Hunger to succeed, to achieve, a hunger to live a lifestyle of our own making and choosing.

The result of that hunger all depends on how hungry you are to change your circumstances and move from your current environment level to the next.

The concept of pain or pleasure underlies success. It is the pain or the pleasure of a circumstance (wish, dream, goal), that gives us the leverage to do something about what it is we want to do something about.

LifeCoaching will give you a clear focus on what your true goals are and a realistic plan of action to realise those wishes. Remember, wishes are empty thoughts until you put some action behind them.

I am not advocating that anything can be achieved. No. I know that life doesn't always hand out a fair deal or supports us in our thoughts and actions. What I am saying is that, all is possible with;

CHAPTER 1 — LifeCoaching

Clarity

    Focus

        Tenacity

            Congruency

                Determination.

When you decide to incorporate these five previously mentioned components then I can say to you that 'everything that both, you and I set out to do can be achieved'.

In other words everything is possible when clarity is abundant, focus is directed, tenacity is applied at all times, congruency flows and determination is on going.

CHAPTER 1 — LifeCoaching

There are many tools used by excellent LifeCoach practitioners. To obtain all of the steps listed on page 4, I would suggest that you employ the masterfulness of the power of The 6 Step Coaching Model, a popular and instantly effective LifeCoaching tool that I will share with you now;

THE 6 STEP COACHING MODEL

You can use the model to coach yourself, to help your friends and family or you may even decide to hire a LifeCoach to take you through the model to your next level.

It was Rudyard Kipling and his poem 'I had six honest serving men' that inspired me to create this simple, yet effective, and progressive coaching model.

Coaching requires rapport from both the LifeCoach and the client in order to put into place quality questions. The 6 Step Coaching Model does just that.

Here are the coaching questions that will allow you to take responsibility for yourself and realise what needs to happen to achieve the desired outcome.

CHAPTER 1 — LifeCoaching

WHAT?   (The clarity question)

What do you want?
What do you really want in order to claim 'success' in your lifestyle?

WHY?   (The congruency question)

Why do you want that?
Why do you need to have that?

WHEN?   (The timeframe question)

When do you need to have it by?
When will you know you have it?

WHERE?   (The focus question)

Where will you be when you have it?
Where will it happen?

CHAPTER 1   LifeCoaching

WHO? (The tenacity question. The question needs to be asked 'does the goal focus on someone else?' In other words what the client would like to have happen for another person, not their own goal)

Who says you need to have it?
Who else will be affected by the achievement of the goal?

HOW? (This question incorporate all of the above)

How will it happen?
How will you begin?
How will you continue?
How will you know you have it?

As you can see I have managed in the space of a few words to establish a simple and on-going device towards true goals, that can be defined and a realistic goal achievement plan of action put into place.

Discover for yourself your core beliefs and live your life congruently.

I invite you to use this model regularly. Use it with respect and let it stand for what you believe to be true

CHAPTER 1   LifeCoaching

THE PRINCIPLES of LiFE COACHING

1. Rapport is the essence of an excellent LifeCoach. Without it trust is non-existent. On-going communication needs to be part of the coaching relationship as well in order to attain measurable results.

    Let's talk about Rapport. This ingredient needs to be built up from the word go. No person is un-approachable or could be termed as resistant.

2. Next comes the creativity bit. The part where we engineer the blue print. This comes from our sensory experiences. A lot of problems or 'challenges' as they are referred to within the concept of LifeCoaching, that individuals experience emanates from what has been put inside of their head by other people. 'The map is not the territory'; so it makes sense to change the thought pattern(s), which in turn nudges the territory.

    I would like to add that no one is a victim of circumstance or his or her environment. What I truly believe is rather each one of us has the ability to think thoughts and believe in those thoughts. They in turn create the occasion and the ability to change the outcome.

CHAPTER 1   LifeCoaching

'If you always do what you've always done, then you'll always have what you always get'. So maybe its about time to do something differently.

3. The outcome, or goal needs to be established. No goal is too big. What it does have to be - is realistic for the present in order to create a pathway towards achieving the whole outcome = the future. Every experience adds to the outcome and should be viewed as an unprecedented opportunity to learn. There is no such thing as 'failure', only a result that wasn't wanted.

4. Utilisation of our current resources. That's what aids results. Use what you have to get what you want. As the saying goes 'Use it or lose it'.

5. The memory bank in humans uses the same neurological circuits as thought. Therefore it's possible that the same impact will happen. So, what one individual can achieve so can another, but of course, differently. In other words the journey to the goal will differ as will the result. But, the method of achievement and tools and techniques and skills could be very similar.

CHAPTER 1   LifeCoaching

A LifeCoach has access to this level of self-development and is able to steer clients towards their preferred standard of lifestyle. Their destiny.

This is a reminder what a LifeCoach will do for you. Together, but elegantly separate, you will explore the self-developing system of LifeCoaching and learn how to take your lifestyle to the next level. You will not regard your LifeCoach as a consultant who maps out your life choices for you. Neither will you look for counsel and advice from your LifeCoach, nor therapy by delving into the past. Rather, your LifeCoach will champion you and coach you to where you want to go within the realistic boundaries you set for yourself.

Today I am your LifeCoach and as you read these pages and begin putting together your personal destiny map, I will do my level best to champion you forward and encourage you to move towards and achieve your goals.

This time is for you; use it wisely to not only discern your goals, but to organise the appropriate LifeCoaching tools you need to put into place and give you the solutions you need as part of your 'blue print'.

Ultimately enjoy the process.

CHAPTER 2   Inspiration and what it means

Inspiration as defined in the dictionary speaks of 'giving rise to', 'creativity'. I too compound those ideas.

Inspiration is that picture impregnated behind your closed eyes, those thoughts in your mind and the degree of measurement that gives you the impetus to do or not to do.

Everyday we follow a routine. We do what we need to do and sometimes we do more. It's that 'more' in life that gives us the edge. How often are you prepared to go the extra mile? To do the 'extra' in 'extra-ordinary'?

To be inspired needs to be a natural development for everyone. But be warned, not to take part in the emotion of being curious. Curiosity did indeed kill the cat. But clever self-questioning can take you from the heat of the moment to back on track of being inspired.

There are many benefits to derive from taking action when inspiration shows up. Obviously extra care needs to be taken when dealing with sensitive issues.

I discovered that a common factor of successful people is that they follow through with their actions. They do this by 'giving rise to' their 'creativity'.

CHAPTER 2   Inspiration and what it means

Perhaps if you were to consistently apply that 'extra' to all that you do, you too would experience an 'extra-ordinary' lifestyle.

Did you know that we only use about 3% to 7% of our brainpower? That means we are losing out on over 90% of success!

Wow, over 90% of brainpower going down the drain. What a waste. Ideally it would be wise to learn how to utilise that other 90%, maybe a little confidence building would be helpful.

To build confidence in self and how to handle what life throws at each of us is being able to remember that up to this point in life you have already achieved a certain amount of success and handled their attainment well. You did that in two ways, one, by interrupting your pattern of thought, and the other by remembering past successes. This *self-modelling* gave you clarity and recognition on how to create your own strategy towards self-confidence.

Self-confidence feeds inspiration and inspiration feeds self-confidence. It's a two way street.

CHAPTER 2   Inspiration and what it means

Inspiration comes to each of us in varying degrees. Gradually as acknowledgement takes place, responsibility of self a deeper understanding of inspiration comes into play, which in turn steadily, gives self-power.

To allow self-power to happen it's important to consciously change your own behaviour. Then the most uncanny situation arises. It is as if by magic others change their behaviour towards you!

Another element of inspiration is awareness. Awareness is the food of inspiration. Think about it. Be logical in your thoughts. By taking the time to consider how aware you are of all that goes on in your world, you will develop your level of inspiration. Now take care and don't become confused with taking responsibility for others. No. Each individual needs to be alert to their own responsibilities in life, that way inspiration will flow and your personal growth will flourish.

Move forward with conviction and you'll probably find that your inspiration will grow enormously as you move towards goal.

I have always believed that daily action enhances lifestyle. To that I can add that daily action encourages inspiration to build.

CHAPTER 2   Inspiration and what it means

LifeCoaching has given me inspiration through the years and I believe that anyone who diligently makes a plan, reviews it daily and follows it through is inspired enough deserve success.

The nuance of self-development is gaining momentum in the external appearance of LifeCoaching. If you would like to take the ideas held within these page forward to the next level either; to hire a LifeCoach or to train as a LifeCoach please click www.lifecoachschoolinternational.co.uk. Or call LifeCoach School international on Bournemouth 01202 389998 and we can discuss your coaching needs, or how you can begin to train as an accredited LifeCoach.

CHAPTER 3 — Insightful expressions

- 1 - 4

Pepper Your Life With Dreams

Today is preparation for the next opportunity.

A happy heart is a light heart.

Don't travel the journey of life alone; take all who will go with you.

Welcome all that will help you to claim success.

CHAPTER 3 — Insightful expressions

- 5 - 8

Pepper Your Life With Dreams

Give yourself a gift every day, no matter how small or how large.

Gift yourself by offering a gift to another.

Poverty encourages togetherness.

Wealth encourages isolation.

CHAPTER 3 — Insightful expressions

- 9 - 12

Before you set sail in your boat, make sure it is rigged in the right direction.

Work towards what you deserve.

Be faithful and do your part.

Congratulate yourself when you know you deserve it.

Pepper Your Life With Dreams

CHAPTER 3   Insightful expressions

- 13 - 16

P
e
p
p
e
r

Step up and then step up again, and again, and again, and again.

Y
o
u
r

Always do the right thing, by your standards.

L
i
f
e

W
i
t
h

Challenges in life are a sign of life.

D
r
e
a
m
s

Only residents in the cemetery don't have challenges. Do you live in the cemetery?

CHAPTER 3 — Insightful expressions

- 17 - 20

There are no problems, only challenges.

Challenges help you to develop your character.

Challenges build your spirituality.

Challenges always allow you to exercise choice.

Pepper Your Life With Dreams

CHAPTER 3 — Insightful expressions

- 21 - 24

Pepper Your Life With Dreams

Repetition builds and build up, builds up.

The biggest problem you will ever have in life is meeting the challenge.

Focus encourages success.

Success encourages focus.

CHAPTER 3 — Insightful expressions

- 25 - 28

Focus and you will succeed.

The key to success is consistency.

Excellence stems from consistency.

Consistency creates results.

Pepper Your Life With Dreams

CHAPTER 3 — Insightful expressions

Pepper Your Life With Dreams

- 29 - 32

Build your self-esteem and underestimate rather then overestimate, that way you will deliver the goods on time.

Reward yourself regularly, you know you deserve it.

No one can take from you what you will not give.

You are your own Lord and Master.

CHAPTER 3 — Insightful expressions

- 33 - 36

Believe in yourself first, and then others will follow.

Every day is an opportunity to make it new again.

Everyday is Today.

Today is the only day we've got.

Pepper Your Life With Dreams

CHAPTER 3   Insightful expressions

- 37 - 40

Pepper Your Life With Dreams

Answer only to your name, nothing less, and nothing more.

Go into the silence daily and build your confidence, this is your strength.

Let your heart live.

A smile makes for a light heart.

CHAPTER 3 — Insightful expressions

- 41 - 44

Where there is a heart there is love.

Your world is yours expand its horizon and live.

Look to the horizon and beyond.

Go for the goal and prosper along the way.

CHAPTER 3 — Insightful expressions

- 45 - 48

Pepper Your Life With Dreams

The journey is the fun bit, so enjoy it.

Life dishes out its fair share of trouble and strife, so don't invite trouble and strife to your front door.

Wade when in deep water, and make sure you know the depth of the waterbed.

Decide what you need and make it happen.

CHAPTER 3 — Insightful expressions

- 49 - 52

Make it happen, and then decide what you need.

Fix your mind and you'll fix your life.

All things are possible when you commit
to do whatever you can possibly do.

Begin with what you have, then carry on with
what you get until you have what you want.

CHAPTER 3 — Insightful expressions

- 53 - 56

Pepper Your Life With Dreams

Only one thing matters, that's you.

Satisfaction is the prize worth working for.

Happiness comes from a pure heart.

A pure heart brings happiness.

CHAPTER 3 — Insightful expressions

- 57 - 60

Set yourself free and choose wisely.

Choose wisely and freedom is yours.

Draw on your inner strengths in moments of sadness.

Give yourself time to rest and recuperate.

Pepper Your Life With Dreams

CHAPTER 3 — Insightful expressions

- 61 - 64

Pepper Your Life With Dreams

Fly with the wind.

Rise with the sun.

You can stop the tide if you want to.

You'll find treasure where your heart is.

CHAPTER 3 — Insightful expressions

- 65 - 68

Learn what you don't know and build on what you do know.

Your personal journey begins today.

Yours personal achievements began when you decided to begin.

It all happens first in your mind, your next step is to take the action towards your personal journey.

Pepper Your Life With Dreams

CHAPTER 3 — Insightful expressions

Pepper Your Life With Dreams

- 69 - 72

To gain insight, go within.

To gain successes keep your focus on the goal.

Your heart is your treasure.

Your heart is all that you need.

CHAPTER 3 — Insightful expressions

- 73 - 76

Wear the clothes that will elicit praise.
Dress to please yourself.

Wear what makes you feel comfortable.

Choose yourself first.

Choose your style.

Pepper Your Life With Dreams

CHAPTER 3 — Insightful expressions

- 77 - 80

Pepper Your Life With Dreams

Pay yourself first.

Always be tax efficient in all financial matters.

Be proud of who you are.

Hold out your hand and receive.

CHAPTER 3 — Insightful expressions

- 81 - 84

Give with both hands.

Bless all that you give out.

Give thanks for all that you receive.

Live in a state of Bliss.

Pepper Your Life With Dreams

CHAPTER 3 — Insightful expressions

- 85 - 88

Pepper Your Life With Dreams

Bliss is yours for the asking.

Ask and you shall receive.

Knock at the door, open it and then go in.

You are your own wealth.

CHAPTER 3 — Insightful expressions

- 89 - 92

Bear fruit in all that you do and success is yours.

Share, and you will receive even more.

Count and respect all that you have,
even the hairs on your head!

Carry only gratitude.

Pepper Your Life With Dreams

CHAPTER 3 — Insightful expressions

- 93 - 96

Pepper Your Life With Dreams

Do not carry any burden,
nor yours or anyone else's.

Drink from the well and feed your lifestyle.

Regularly water your garden of life.

Create your own success and then help
others to create their success.

CHAPTER 3 — Insightful expressions

- 97 - 100

Pepper Your Life With Dreams

There is no such thing as failure, only another opportunity to do it again differently.

Success is what you believe it to be.

Live in a state of success.

Banish poverty from your lifestyle.

CHAPTER 3 — Insightful expressions

- 101 - 104

Pepper Your Life With Dreams

Keep your joy by sharing it.

Choose your way and follow it.

Change direction when you need to.

Review your goals, daily.

CHAPTER 3   Insightful expressions

- 105 - 108

Pepper Your Life With Dreams

Peace is beautiful, be beautiful.

Live simply and you will have it all.

Remember your promises.

Everyday you are with yourself,
until the end of time.

CHAPTER 3 — Insightful expressions

- 109 - 112

Pepper Your Life With Dreams

Stop then begin again.

Every day brings a new challenge.

Every day allows each and all of us to re-new a passion for living.

The following simple question actually inspires me to shake off the doldrums and do something, when I feel low.

CHAPTER 3 — Insightful expressions

- 113 - 116

'What can I do right now to achieve
a WIN WIN outcome?'

WIN WIN is what you decide the result is,
not the result you believe you will get.

Without it, whatever it is, I wouldn't
have known I had it.

Life throws up little incidences.

Pepper Your Life With Dreams

CHAPTER 3 — Insightful expressions

Pepper Your Life With Dreams

- 117 - 120

Every action gives birth to a reaction.

Boundaries add to the quality of life, put them in place and enjoy unlimited space.

Open the door and let whom you want come in. Otherwise keep the door firmly shut.

Do you love yourself?

CHAPTER 3 — Insightful expressions

- 121 - 124

Let light in and keep darkness out.

Believe that anything is possible and your faith will make it happen.

As an adult become a child.

As a child become an adult.

Pepper Your Life With Dreams

CHAPTER 3 — Insightful expressions

- 125 - 128

Pepper Your Life With Dreams

Your imagination is your key to success.

It's only your imagination that keeps you from moving forward.

Be faithful to your imagination.

Ignore liars.

CHAPTER 3 — Insightful expressions

- 129 - 132

Ignore gossip.

Laugh, it's outrageously contagious.

If you think about it, you'll find you already have the key to the lock.

If you do something about it, you definitely have the key to the lock.

Pepper Your Life With Dreams

CHAPTER 3 — Insightful expressions

- 133 - 136

Pepper

With determination put the key into the lock and open the door.

Your

Begin at the beginning and move on to the finish line.

Life

Be strong, find a role model and learn what you don't know,

With

Be still and enjoy the peace.

Dreams

CHAPTER 3 — Insightful expressions

- 137 - 140

Excellence is the ultimate.

Forget about the word 'can't'; instead go for 'can'.

Hope is good, focus is a lot better.

Wish yourself good luck every day.

Pepper Your Life With Dreams

CHAPTER 3 — Insightful expressions

- 141 - 144

Pepper Your Life With Dreams

Rise in the morning, work in the day,
and rest at night.

The tools of life are already within your tool bag,
open it now and create what you truly desire.

Perfection is not the goal, rather excellence.

Being human is no excuse for procrastination.

CHAPTER 3 — Insightful expressions

- 145 - 148

> Humanity is OK. It's all the other people that spoil it.

> Wonders are there for all of us, go and experience yours.

> Be your own best friend.

> To be slim is to exercise choice. Eat like a King for breakfast. Eat as a Prince at lunch. Dine as a pauper.

Pepper Your Life With Dreams

CHAPTER 3 — Insightful expressions

- 149 - 152

Pepper

Instruct yourself and gather the data necessary to move your lifestyle forward.

Your

Observe cats, see how graceful they are, and be graceful in all that you do.

Life

Dogs are loving and loyal. Are you?

With

Dreams

Live your life as honestly as you know you should.

CHAPTER 3 — Insightful expressions

- 153 - 156

Listen to what you say.

Take action on what you say.

When in the dark move into the light.

Gratitude is the essence of receiving more.

Pepper Your Life With Dreams

CHAPTER 3 — Insightful expressions

- 157 - 160

Pepper Your Life With Dreams

Whatever you ask for, believe that it will be yours and so shall it be.

Don't mark time you'll waste it, instead use it wisely.

Goodness is that feeling of sharing.

Achievement is that feeling of sharing goodness.

CHAPTER 3 — Insightful expressions

- 161 - 164

Dust has a sneaky way of creeping
in everyday. Get rid of it.

Keep on Keeping on.

Take the plunge and see how far it is.

Keep on Keeping on, except when a bus is
coming straight at you, then go around.

Pepper Your Life With Dreams

CHAPTER 3 — Insightful expressions

- 165 - 168

Pepper Your Life With Dreams

Love and laughter make merry. Make merry and have love and laughter.

Do I know what you know?

Do you know what I know?

Knowing is power and power is knowing!

CHAPTER 3 — Insightful expressions

- 169 - 172

Good friends are few and far between.
Cherish your friendships.

Make no sound until it's done.

Tell no one your true dreams.

Focus your energy on the task in hand.

Pepper Your Life With Dreams

CHAPTER 3   Insightful expressions

- 173 - 176

Pepper Your Life With Dreams

At eventide, don't despair; it'll be all right in the morning.

Always be yourself life isn't a stage.

If people can't accept you for who you are, they are not worth knowing.

Don't spend unnecessary energy and waste your time.

CHAPTER 3 Insightful expressions

- 177 - 180

Remember, there are 24 hours in a day.

Never change for anyone, always be yourself.

You are who you are. Accept it.

Raise your standards. Then keep them raised.

Pepper Your Life With Dreams

CHAPTER 3 — Insightful expressions

- 181 - 184

Pepper Your Life With Dreams

You can be whatever you want to be,
if you put your mind to it.

Forget your failures, remember and
focus on your achievements.

Decide who you want to be and be YOU.

Misfortune only appears when you seek it.

CHAPTER 3 — Insightful expressions

- 185 - 188

Fortune appears when you seek it.

Life is a game, play to win.

As you play the game of life, play it with elegance.

Do not become weighted by your failures, rather be positive and have weight.

Pepper Your Life With Dreams

CHAPTER 3 — Insightful expressions

- 189 - 192

P
e
p
p
e
r

You attract what you are.
So be what you want to be.

Y
o
u
r   Don't put a guard up; instead be on your guard.

L
i
f
e

W   Welcome with open arms.
i
t
h

D
r
e   Smile.
a
m
s

CHAPTER 3 — Insightful expressions

- 193 - 196

Pepper Your Life With Dreams

Enjoy.

Look for the best in all.

Laugh.

It takes 16 incorrect inputs to replace a correct input.

CHAPTER 3 — Insightful expressions

- 197 - 200

Pepper Your Life With Dreams

Make your input worthwhile.

Decide to be positive.

Build your confidence from within.

You deserve it.

CHAPTER 3   Insightful expressions

- 201 - 204

Don't you?

What? Is the question. It can also the answer.

Are people treating you as you treat them?

Tell yourself 'I am beautiful, inside and out'.

CHAPTER 3   **Insightful expressions**

- 205 - 208

Pepper Your Life With Dreams

Have you got CBA?

CBA Conceive it. Believe it. Achieve it.

Believe in yourself and life will be all
that you want it to be.

Bank what you don't spend.

CHAPTER 3 — Insightful expressions

- 209 - 212

Spend your time wisely.

Shore up your energy.

Appreciate all that you can see around you.

Another day, another opportunity.

Pepper Your Life With Dreams

CHAPTER 3 — Insightful expressions

- 213 - 216

P
e
p
p
e
r

Understand and you will be understood.

Y
o
u
r

Hold true feelings in your heart.

L
i
f
e

W The future holds no promises, but make your
i promises and keep them.
t
h

D
r
e Success is yours for the asking. Ask.
a
m
s

CHAPTER 3   **Insightful expressions**

- 217 - 220

Pepper Your Life With Dreams

Faith, hope and charity are core principles.
Do you have these principles?

Follow your dreams.

Pepper your life with dreams and
add a little spice to your life.

Determine what you want and then
go after it with determination.

CHAPTER 3 — Insightful expressions

- 221 - 224

P
e
p
p	Live up to a challenge every day.
e
r

Y
o
u	Have pride in what you do.
r

L
i
f
e

W	Do all that you do, with pride.
i
t
h

D
r
e	Always give something to someone else,
a	a smile, a flower, and a prayer.
m
s

CHAPTER 3 — Insightful expressions

- 225 - 228

Pepper Your Life With Dreams

Fill up your life with laughter.

Always live your life to make a difference.

Speak with kindness.

Be gentle with others.

CHAPTER 3 — Insightful expressions

- 229 - 232

Pepper Your Life With Dreams

Be gentle with yourself.

Allow others to show gentleness towards you.

Do you know who you are? Find out.

Aim for success and achieve success.

CHAPTER 3 — Insightful expressions

- 233 - 236

Do you genuinely 'go the extra mile'?

Take your courage in both hands
and move forward.

Be strong and build your weaknesses
into strength.

Change when change is for your higher self.

Pepper Your Life With Dreams

CHAPTER 3   Insightful expressions

- 237 - 240

Pepper Your Life With Dreams

Dreams can come true.
(I challenge you to prove me wrong)

Dream your dreams and dream
them true with action.

Create success.

Live success.

CHAPTER 3   Insightful expressions

- 241 - 244

Don't even think about the failings of the past you will only hinder living successfully in the present.

Enjoy what you have and decide to improve what you have.

Build your self-esteem by distancing yourself from any outcomes you consider to be a failure.

To accept policies of others is OK; just ask yourself if others can accept your policies?

Pepper Your Life With Dreams

CHAPTER 3   Insightful expressions

- 245 - 248

Pepper Your Life With Dreams

Build quality boundaries around you,
that way you'll always have quality.

Earn money by working at what you really enjoy.

Save 50% of your income and spend the
remaining 50% on humanity.

Increase your abundance by giving abundance.

CHAPTER 3 — Insightful expressions

- 249 - 252

Protect what is yours and respect
what is not yours.

Some rules were made to be broken,
choose wisely.

Evaluate all the procedures you follow otherwise
you will follow valueless procedures.

Create lasting change within your lifestyle
by being consistent.

Pepper Your Life With Dreams

CHAPTER 3   Insightful expressions

- 253 - 256

Pepper Your Life With Dreams

When you hit the jackpot, share it!

Always ask quality questions, that way you'll receive quality answers.

Don't take advantage, give the advantage.

To change what you have got change your attitude.

CHAPTER 3 — Insightful expressions

- 157 - 260

Pepper Your Life With Dreams

To keep what you have got, live your attitude.

When in pain, don't, instead do something painless.

When in grief, 'do', and then move on.

Accept your weaknesses and improve them by recognising your strengths.

CHAPTER 3 — Insightful expressions

- 261 - 264

Pepper Your Life With Dreams

Go for gold and develop your
Positive Mental Attitude.

Always be honest with yourself
and with all you meet.

Don't be foolish about your reality,
just be honest.

Work smart, not hard.

CHAPTER 3 — Insightful expressions

- 265 - 268

Reward yourself with praise on a job well done.

By being happy you are developing your trust.

Always go that little bit further,
you know that you can.

What you believe yourself to
be that is what you are.

Pepper Your Life With Dreams

CHAPTER 3 — Insightful expressions

- 269 - 272

Pepper Your Life With Dreams

Leave a legacy.

Are you extra-ordinary?

Do you know what the difference
is in your lifestyle?

Look forward every day to miracles,
you can make them happen.

CHAPTER 3 — Insightful expressions

- 273 - 276

Do you know why you are here?

Do you know why you are reading this book?

I'm going to challenge you again. 'I challenge you to find the solution to your dreams'.

That challenge is so powerful I know it will start you on your road to success.

Pepper Your Life With Dreams

CHAPTER 3 — Insightful expressions

- 277 - 280

Pepper Your Life With Dreams

It will help you to make decisions that are relevant and important to make your dreams come true.

With that I urge you to make the decision to have an even higher level of commitment to do two things;

Power stems from within, unlock it now.

Welcome all that will help you to grow.

CHAPTER 3 — Insightful expressions

- 281 - 284

Focus encourages growth.

Growth encourages focus.

Focus and grow.

Be strong, find a role model and learn what you don't know.

Pepper Your Life With Dreams

CHAPTER 3 — Insightful expressions

- 285 - 289

Pepper Your Life With Dreams

Goodness is that feeling of sharing.

Achievement is that feeling of sharing goodness.

Music is inspiration for my journey.

First promise yourself that you will review your goals daily.

Second that you will Pepper Your Life With Dreams.

TRAINING

Your opportunity to learn the craft of LifeCoaching.

I have enjoyed sharing with you a few of my ideas and thoughts and a selection of tools available within the new and exciting industry of LifeCoaching. And as I have said earlier, the nuance of self-development is gaining momentum in the external appearance of LifeCoaching.

Therefore, if you would like to take the ideas held within these pages forward to the next level and train as a LifeCoach please click;

www.lifecoachschoolinternational.co.uk.

Or telephone LifeCoach School international on Bournemouth 01202 389998 to discuss how you can begin your training as an accredited LifeCoach.

COACHING LEADS TO SUCCESS

Looking forward to early 2003 another title by PaTrisha Anne.

LifeCoaching A-Z   ISBN 0-9543262-1-0